IT'S ELECTRIC!

Using Electricity

T0100931

Chris Oxlade

Heinemann Library
Chicago, Illinois

www.capstonepub.com
Visit our website to find out more information about Heinemann-Raintree books.

To order:
Phone 800-747-4992
Visit www.capstonepub.com to browse our catalog and order online.

© 2012 Heinemann Library
an imprint of Capstone Global Library, LLC
Chicago, Illinois

All rights reserved. No part of this publication may be reproduced or transmitted in any form or by any means, electronic or mechanical, including photocopying, recording, taping, or any information storage retrieval system, without permission in writing from the publisher.

Edited by Daniel Nunn, Rebecca Rissman, and Catherine Veitch
Designed by Joanna Hinton-Malivoire
Picture research by Elizabeth Alexander
Production by Eirian Griffiths
Originated by Capstone Global Library, Ltd.

Library of Congress Cataloging-in-Publication Data
Oxlade, Chris.
Using electricity / Chris Oxlade.
p. cm.—(It's electric!)
Includes bibliographical references and index.
ISBN 978-1-4329-5676-9 (hb)—ISBN 978-1-4329-5681-3 (pb) 1. Electricity—Juvenile literature. I. Title.
TK148.O96 2012
621.3—dc23 2011016537

Acknowledgments
The author and publisher are grateful to the following for permission to reproduce photographs: Alamy pp. 26 (© PhotoAlto), 27 (© GIPhotoStock X), 29 (© Ted Foxx); © Capstone Publishers p. 18 (Karon Dubke); iStockphoto pp. 12 (© Gene Chutka), 23 (© ricardoazoury), 24 (© Andrew Howe), 25 (© Torsten Stahlberg); Shutterstock pp. 4 (© Sherri R. Camp), 5 (© sevenke), 6 (© Roger De Marfa), 7 (© yampi), 8 (© Rafa Irusta), 9 (© Chungking), 10 (© prism68), 11 (© Elena Elisseeva), 13 (© Discpicture), 14 (© Erzetic), 15 left (© Sideways Design), 15 right (© Esbobeldijk), 16 (© J van der Wolf), 17 (© Songquan Deng), 19 (© Tatiana Popova), 20 (© Grandpa), 21 (© Karnizz), 22 © Baloncici), 28 (© Katharina Wittfeld).

Cover photograph of a harbor laser light show in Hong Kong reproduced with permission of Shutterstock (© markrhiggins). Design background feature reproduced with permission of Shutterstock (© echo3005).

The publisher would like to thank John Pucek for his assistance in the preparation of this book.

Every effort has been made to contact copyright holders of material reproduced in this book. Any omissions will be rectified in subsequent printings if notice is given to the publisher.

Disclaimer
All the Internet addresses (URLs) given in this book were valid at the time of going to press. However, due to the dynamic nature of the Internet, some addresses may have changed or ceased to exist since publication. While the author and publisher regret any inconvenience this may cause readers, no responsibility for any such changes can be accepted by either the author or the publisher.

Printed in the United States 4780

Contents

Using Electricity 4
Electricity and Energy 6
Making Electricity 8
Electricity Supply 10
Electricity at Home 12
Electric Light 14
Light for Signs. 16
Batteries 18
Electric Transportation. 20
Electricity in Industry 22
Electronics 24
Saving Electricity 26
Safe with Electricity 28
Glossary 30
Find Out More 31
Index 32

Some words are shown in bold, **like this**. You can find them in the glossary on page 30.

Using Electricity

Take a look around the room you are in. How many things in the room work using electricity? Count the ones that use **batteries** as well as household electricity. Don't forget the lights!

Every day of our lives we use many electric machines. We use them at home, at school, at work, and in factories. It would be impossible to live our lives without electricity.

Electricity and Energy

Electricity makes things work. It makes the motors in a washing machine spin, it makes music players give out sound, and it makes televisions show pictures. Electricity is a type of **energy**.

Electricity is a really useful type of energy. This is because we can change it into light, movement, or heat. Light, movement, and heat are types of energy, too.

An electric stove turns electricity into heat.

Making Electricity

Most electricity is made at power plants. Here, energy is turned into electricity. Electricity is also made at **wind farms**, at **solar power stations**, and at **hydroelectric power stations**.

Electricity travels along thick cables from power plants to towns and cities. The cables are called power lines.

Electricity Supply

Most homes have electricity that comes from power plants. The electricity reaches homes along cables, often under the ground. Schools, offices, factories, and other buildings also get electricity in this way.

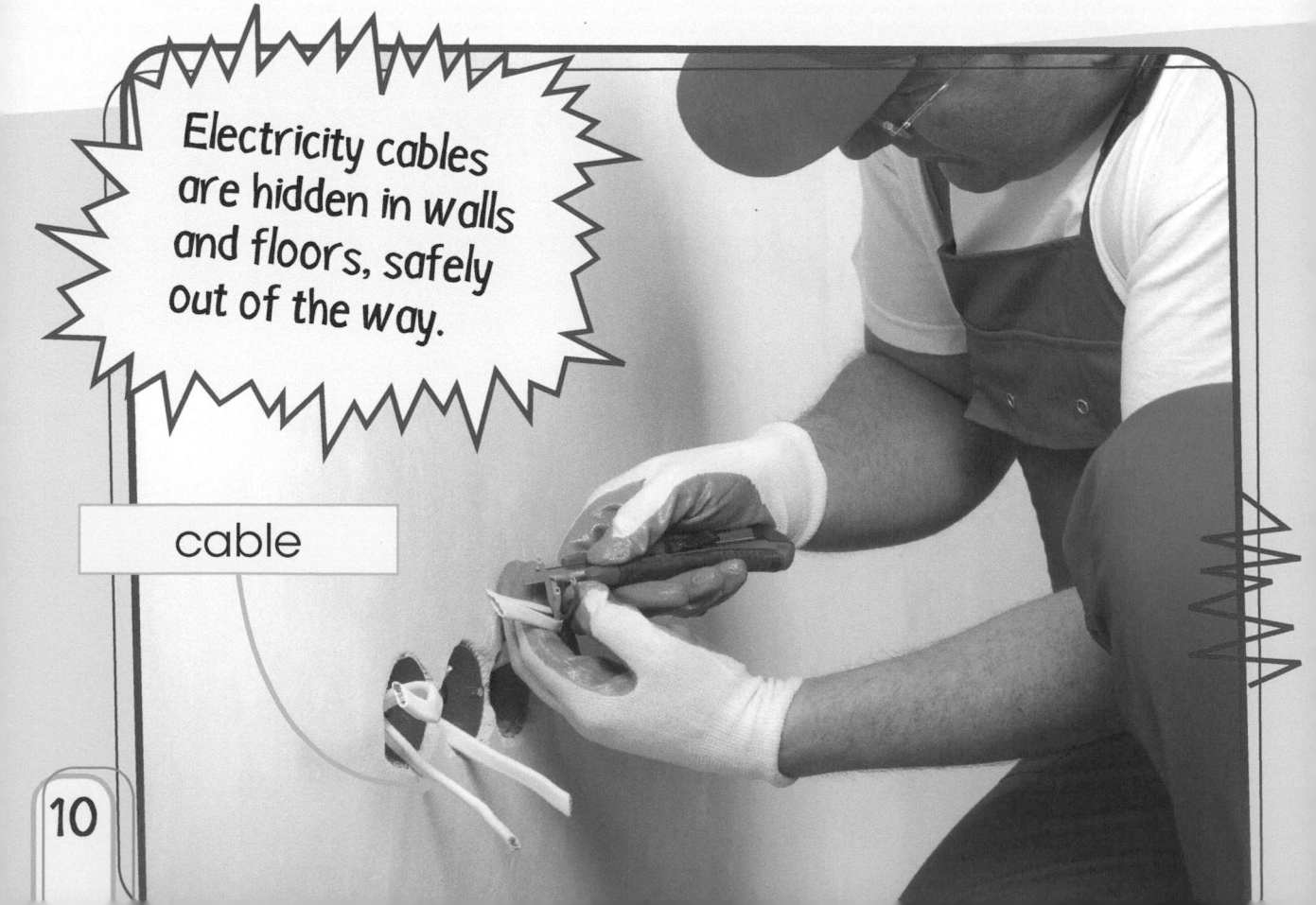

More cables carry the electricity to wall outlets in each room in a home. When you push a plug into an outlet, electricity can flow. Cables also carry electricity to light switches and fixtures.

Electricity can flow when a plug is pushed into an outlet.

Electricity at Home

Electricity powers game consoles and televisions.

Electricity works many appliances and gadgets in our homes. It powers televisions, computers, radios, music players, and DVD players. It also powers cleaning and cooking machines.

Electricity does different jobs in many appliances. In a washing machine, it works the motor that turns the drum. It works the heater that heats the water, and it works the pump that gets rid of dirty water.

A washing machine washes clothes using the energy in electricity.

Electric Light

We can turn electric lights on and off with the flick of a switch. Lights let us work and play indoors when it's dark. They also light up our streets, sidewalks, and stadiums.

Light bulbs turn electricity into light. The most common kinds of light bulbs we use in our homes are LED bulbs and compact fluorescent lamps. LED is short for **light-emitting diode**. These bulbs do not use a lot of energy, so they last a long time.

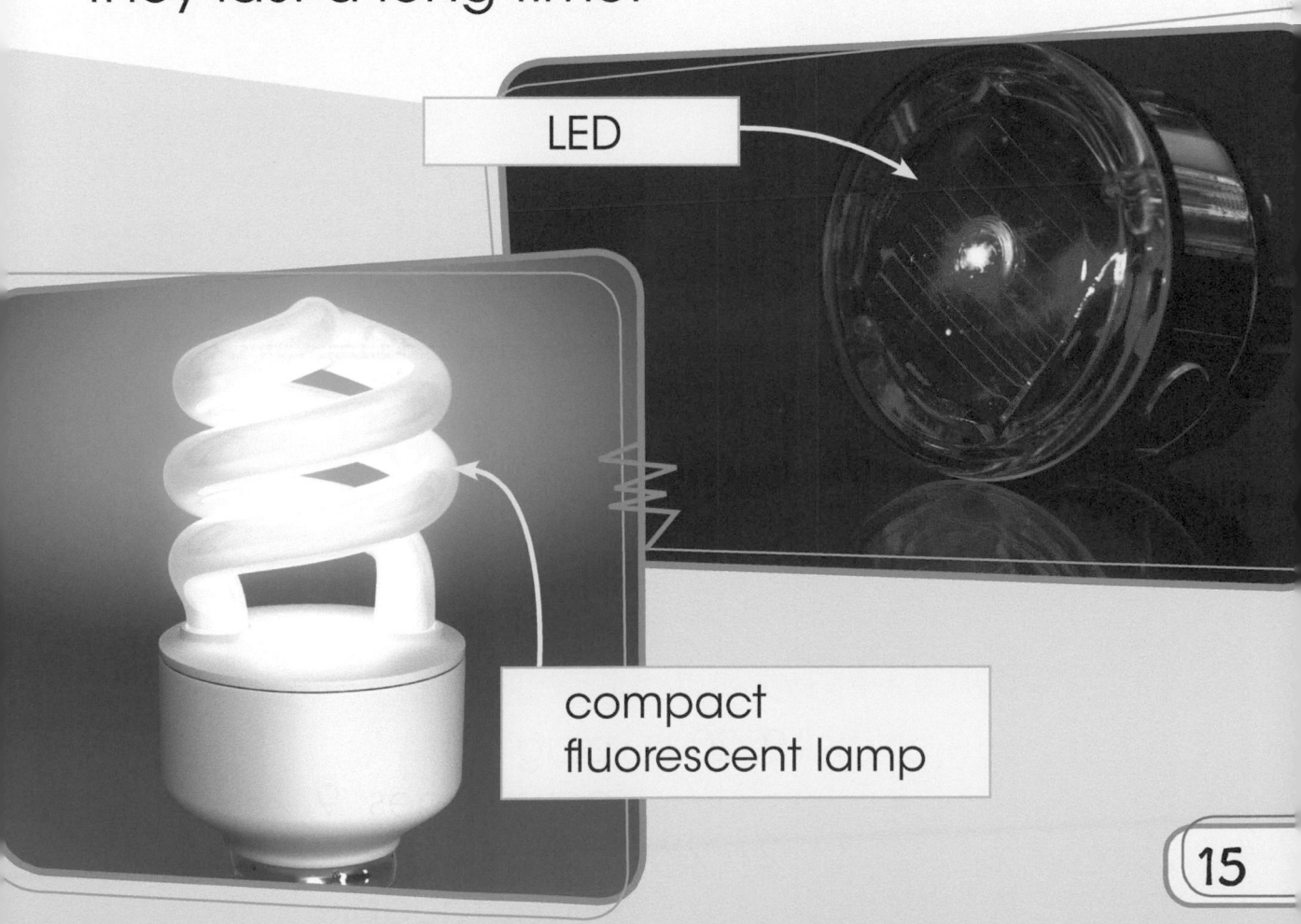

Light for Signs

Colored lights tell drivers when to stop and go.

We use electric lights for giving people information as well as for lighting up rooms. For example, small colored **LEDs** tell us when a machine is switched on, or has finished doing its job.

Electronic billboards are made up of LEDs. They give us information at railway stations and on buses. Lighting up different bulbs makes letters, numbers, and patterns.

Batteries

We use batteries to power toys, phones, and other gadgets, and even electric vehicles. The **batteries** push electricity around an electric circuit. An electric **circuit** is a loop that electricity can flow around.

After a while all of the electricity in a battery is used up. When standard batteries are empty they must be thrown away. **Rechargeable** batteries can be refilled with electricity.

Electric Transportation

Many sorts of transportation use electricity. Electric cars have large **batteries**. The batteries work an electric motor that turns the car's wheels. Electric wheelchairs also have batteries and motors.

Electric trains are moved by powerful electric motors. Some get electricity from a cable above the track. Trams and trolleys also work using electricity from cables above the streets.

Electricity in Industry

Factories need lots of electricity. Electric motors work machines that cut and shape materials such as metals and plastics. They also power machines such as conveyor belts that move materials.

In a car factory, electricity works the tools that workers use to put cars together. Electricity also powers robots that glue the pieces of the cars' bodies together. Electricity lights and heats the factory, too.

Electronics

Machines and gadgets such as computers, calculators, cameras, and mobile telephones have very complicated electric **circuits**. The circuits are called electronic circuits.

There are hundreds of complicated electronic circuits inside a computer.

Electronics control what a machine does. For example, in a calculator the circuits do adding and subtracting and show answers on a display.

A robot vacuum cleaner cleans a room on its own! It is controlled by electronics.

Saving Electricity

Most electricity is made by burning materials called **fossil fuels** in power plants. Burning fuels is not good for our environment. If we use less electricity, we will do less damage. It also means we won't run out of fuel so quickly.

Modern electric machines are made so they use as little electricity as possible while they do their jobs. We say they are **energy-efficient** machines.

Safe with Electricity

Household electricity is very powerful. If it goes through a person, it can badly injure them. The electricity in power lines and in overhead cables on railways is even more dangerous. It can even kill a person.

Never play with household electricity. Never push anything into an electric outlet or into a light fixture. Never take apart any electric machine or gadget. Then you won't get an electric shock.

Glossary

battery part that pushes electricity around a circuit

circuit loop that electricity flows around

energy something that can make things happen. Electricity, light, heat, and sound are all types of energy.

energy efficient machine that uses as little electricity as possible

fossil fuel material that is burnt to make heat, light, or power. Fossil fuels include wood, gas, oil, and coal.

hydroelectric power station place where electricity is made from the energy in flowing water

light-emitting diode (LED) small device that gives out light when electricity flows through it

rechargeable battery that can have electricity put back into it, so it can be used again

solar power station place where electricity is made from the energy in sunshine

wind farm place where electricity is made from the wind using wind turbines

Find Out More

Books

Mullins, Matt. *Electricity (True Books)*. New York: Scholastic, 2011.

Royston, Angela. *Using Electricity (My World of Science)*. Chicago: Heinemann Raintree, 2008.

Weber, Rebecca. *The Power of Energy.* Mankato, Minn.: Capstone, 2011.

Websites

www1.eere.energy.gov/kids/
Find out more ways to save energy at home.

www.eia.gov/kids/energy.cfm?page=electricity_home-basics-k.cfm
Learn more about electricity from this website.

www.engineeringinteract.org/interact.htm
Fun electricity games from Cambridge University (click on Silicon Spies).

Index

batteries 4, 18, 19, 20

cables 9, 10, 11, 21, 28, 29
circuits 18, 24, 25
compact fluorescent lamps 15

energy 6, 7, 8, 13, 15, 27
energy-efficient 27

LEDs 15, 16, 17
lights 4, 11, 14, 15, 16, 23, 29

motors 6, 13, 20, 21, 22

outlets 11, 29

plug 11
power lines 9, 28

rechargeable batteries 19
robots 23, 25

signs 16, 17, 28
switches 11, 14, 29

transmission towers 9

wind turbines 8